Angels Tell The Story
The Cradle, The Cross, The Crown

Published by Shepherd Ministries. Scripture from the New International Version.
Printed in the United States of America

Angels Tell The Story
The Cradle, The Cross, The Crown

Joyfully retold by Barbara Macdonald

Illustrated by Janie Cavender

Special thanks to Al Macdonald
for invaluable input,
to Julie Brzozowski
for initial encouragement,
and to Terry Werntz
for selected artwork.

III

Let's pretend that you wanted to hear for yourself how the angels might tell the STORY.

So you jumped into your Time Machine And zoomed back through time

2,000 Years

1.

You went all the way to the courts of Heaven
just as a loudspeaker was booming out
an announcement:

Gabriel
has called a special
choir practice
All musicians
please report to the
choir room
at O:2OO

At 0:200, the choir room was buzzing with excitment when **Gabriel**, one of God's mightiest Angels, appeared.

3.

"We have been commisioned to announce a Royal Birth!
So I've written a new Anthem."

4.

"A Royal Birth?"
Will we be going to a king's palace?"

5.

Gabriel smiled, "No, we'll be making this announcement to some shepherds who are on a hillside outside the town of Bethlehem."

He continued, "I have just come back from visiting a young Jewish maiden named Mary.
I told her she is highly favored by God and would have a child, a son, a Royal Son.

7.

I had to say "Do not be afraid" because I was wearing my

LED Light Robe and Wings,

so she would know I was a messenger from GOD."

8.

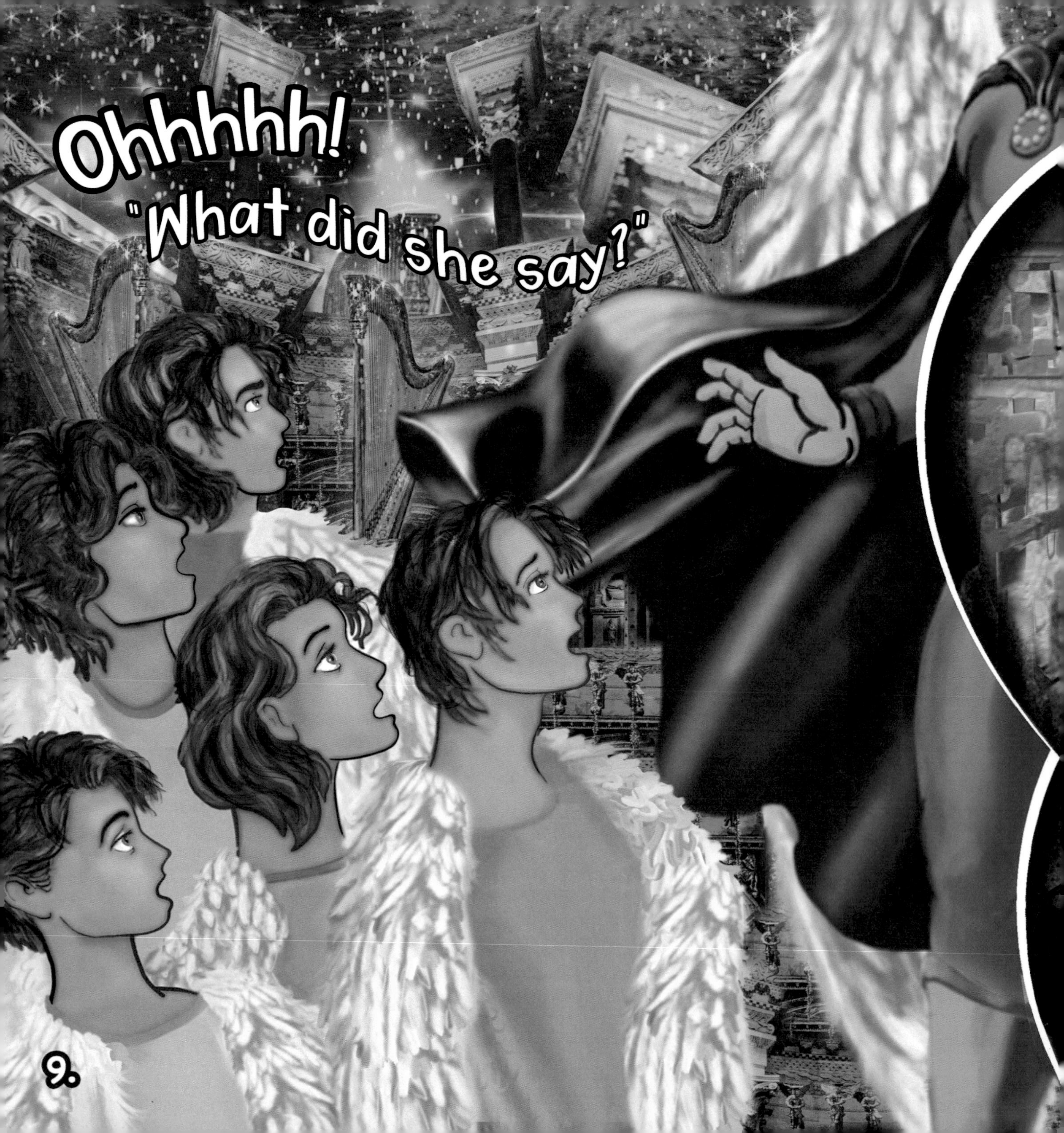
Ohhhhh!
"What did she say?"

10.

"Well then," the angels wondered,
"who will be the father of the child?
Will it be someone great
like Abraham or one of the prophets?"

Gabriel answered,
"There will be no earthly father.
There has never been a birth like this before
or will ever be again!

It will be a miracle ...a Virgin Birth!

11.

The Father will be...THE LORD GOD."

Ohhhhhh!
And the Child?   Then who will the Child be?

Gabriel paused.
"The child will be our beloved Prince.
He will be named..."

JESUS

The Angels were stunned.

"Our Prince?"
The Son of the Most High God?
The Creator of the Universe?

He would give up all of Heaven
to be born as a human?

But humans cannot fly yet.
They have to walk everywhere they go.
And they don't even have

sneakers!

How can this be, Gabriel?"

"It is because God loves all people so much," Gabriel explained. "He knew the only way for them to be saved would be to send his Son.

You know that old devil, Lucifer, along with his Gang, who used to be on our team?

He has been attacking everyone on earth ever since he was kicked out of Heaven

for boasting he would take God's place."

"People need Jesus!"

15.

"Then, if he's going to earth," the angels all agreed,

"the people will love him like we do.

We will find a way to get him some

He can wear them under his robe."

Gabriel smiled at the idea but said sadly,

"No, most people will not love him.
He will lead a sinless life, teach God's Word,
and do many wonderful miracles for them.

But, they will not listen to him or accept him as
the Son of God.
In fact, they will have him crucified."

"HE GAVE UP ALL OF THIS

to humble himself,
and to die on a cross to save them."

17.

18.

NO WAIT!! HERE'S THE BEST PART!

He will triumph over death

and RISE FROM THE TOMB

on the third day!

Then, less than two months later,
He will come back to Heaven to us

and be seated
at the RIGHT HAND OF GOD, HIS FATHER.

HIS MISSION COMPLETE

"Now you know what all the excitement's about. So let's sing this new anthem!"

21.

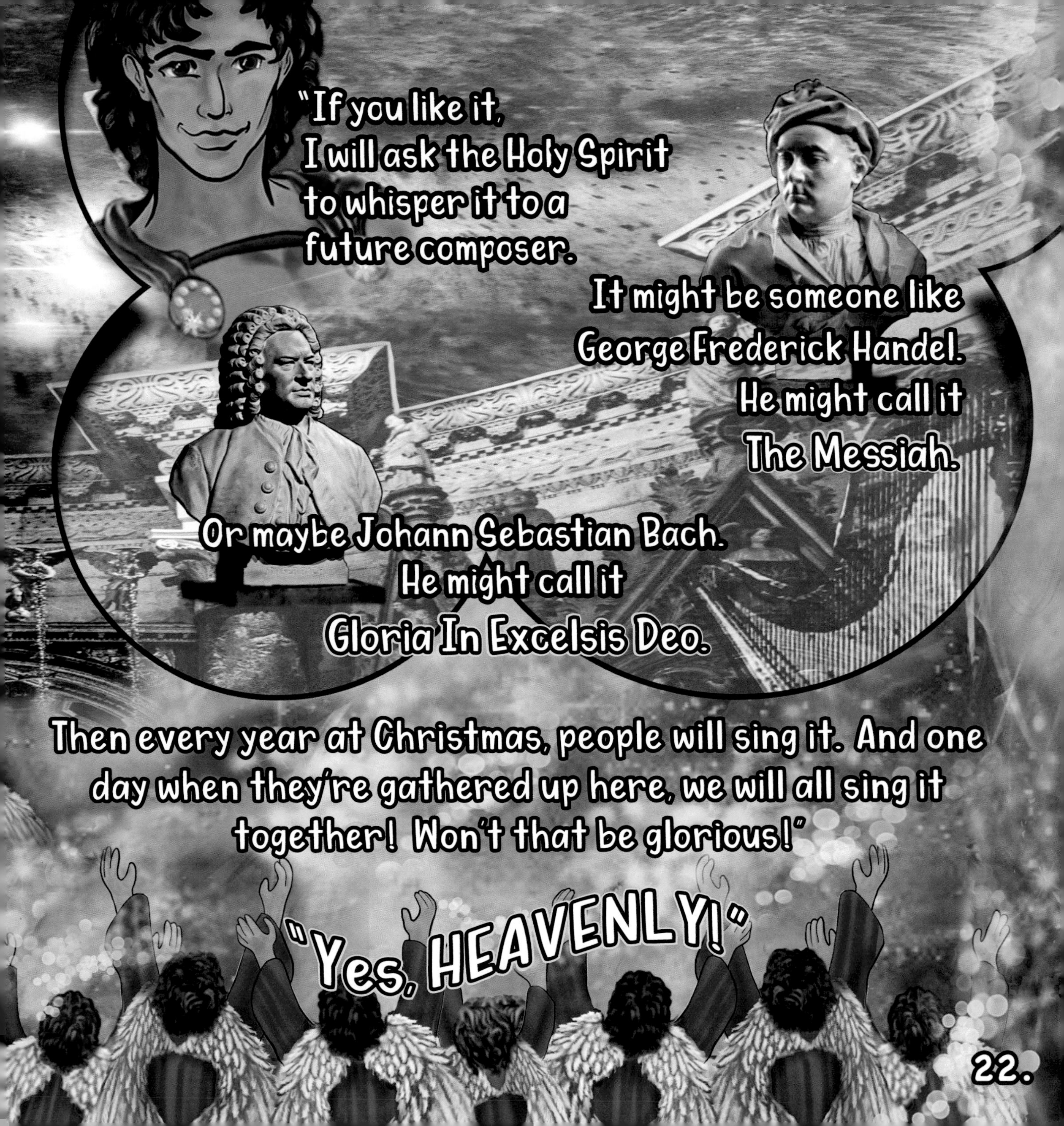

"If you like it,
I will ask the Holy Spirit
to whisper it to a
future composer.

It might be someone like
George Frederick Handel.
He might call it
The Messiah.

Or maybe Johann Sebastian Bach.
He might call it
Gloria In Excelsis Deo.

Then every year at Christmas, people will sing it. And one day when they're gathered up here, we will all sing it together! Won't that be glorious!"

"Yes, HEAVENLY!"

"Let's get ready for the big announcement of THE BIRTH OF JESUS.

You will need to wear your
LED Light Robes and Wings."

24.

Wow!

You were so excited you ran back to the Time Machine and zoomed forward to tell us the Story.

Someone said to you,

"Oh REALLY ? !
LED LIGHT ROBES
AND ?!?"

You smiled and said,
"You can read the story
in the Bible yourself.
Luke chapters I and 2."

Maybe there are no

But GOD'S WORD is a treasure chest!

27.

And it gives us THE REST OF THE STORY...

28

Therefore GOD has highly exalted Him
and given Him a name
that is above every name,
that at the name of JESUS
every knee shall bow.

29.

The Cradle.
The Cross.
The Crown.

The End.

30.

For additional books

AngelsTellTheStory.com
or
Amazon.com

Soft Cover
$12.95 each
Package of 3 books for $35.00
Free Shipping*

Hard Cover
$17.95 each
Package of 3 books for $50.00
Free Shipping*

***If purchased through AngelsTellTheStory.com**

Screen Visuals
Available for Group Presentation
no cost, Drop Box delivery

AngelsTellTheStory.com

Addendum

FAQ's

Frequently Asked Questions about words or statements
that provide an opportunity for discussion
See also on AngelsTellTheStory.com

Cover

1. What Story?
This is about God's great story of love to us. And even though the story actually started in Genesis, this book tells about the time when Jesus was born and lived on earth.

Page 1 and 2

1. 2,000 Years?
We live in the 21st Century. (20_ _) Jesus was born before the year 1 (4-6 BC). That's about 2,000 years give or take a loop around the stars in your Time Machine.

Page 3 and 4

1. Do Angels really look like the ones in the book?
No, they don't really look like the friendly guys in this book or like the ones we see on greeting cards or in other books...that mostly look like girls with wings or flying babies.

What we know about angels is that they are powerful heavenly beings, always described as masculine in scripture, are superior to humans, and given jobs that humans can't do. Angels serve God as His messengers and are ministering spirits and protectors of people who love Him, especially children. *(Psalm 91:9-11, Matthew 18:10)* They are so awesome that nearly every time they appear in scripture, the people are frightened and the angel has to tell them--"BE NOT AFRAID!" Some time when you have a few minutes, read about angels. You'll find them in Genesis, Isaiah, Psalms, Ezekiel, Daniel, the Gospels, and Revelation.

2. How do we know Gabriel's name?
Luke 1:19 and Luke 1:26 tell us that the angel Gabriel was God's messenger of good news. He was sent from God to a city of Galilee named Nazareth, to a virgin whose name was Mary."

3. What is an Anthem?
An Anthem is music that is rousing or uplifting. The Star Spangled Banner is our national anthem celebrating America. Usually it's a composition based on a biblical passage that lifts our hearts in worship of God.

Page 5 and 6

1. **Why would the angels make the announcement outside the town of Bethlehem?**
   Bethlehem was the city where Jesus was born. Mary and Joseph traveled there because of a decree from Caesar Augustus that everyone had to go to their family's home town to register for a census. So Joseph and Mary went up from the town of Nazareth in Galilee, where they lived, to Judea to the town of Bethlehem, called the city of David, because Joseph was a descendant of King David.

   What many do not realize, though, is that this was done to fulfill a prophecy made hundreds of years earlier. Micah 5:2 says: *"But you, Bethlehem Ephrathah, though you are little among the thousands of Judah, yet out of you shall come forth to Me the One to be Ruler in Israel, Whose goings forth are from of old, from everlasting."*

Page 7 and 8

1. **How old was Mary?**
   Mary was a teenager, maybe 13 or 14 years old from a poor family who lived in the town of Nazareth in Galilee. As was the custom in those days, she was pledged or engaged at that young age to be married in the coming year to a man named Joseph.

   Mary was an ordinary girl but she loved God and had an obedient spirit. God saw her heart and chose her to be the mother of His Son and to raise him according to His will.

2. **Why would Mary be afraid when she saw Gabriel?**
   Imagine how she felt when she saw this powerful angel appear out of nowhere whose clothes may have gleamed like lightening. *(Luke 24:4)*

Page 9 and 10

1. **How could Mary have a child if she was a virgin?**
   How could she have this royal son since she had no physical union with her fiancee Joseph that would make it humanly possible for a baby to be born. But this was proof of her love for God and her obedient spirit, because she said "I am the Lord's servant, may it be to me as you have said."

Page 11 and 12

1. **Why was the birth of Jesus a miracle?**
   So if there was no earthly or human father, how could God be the father?   Our great God can do anything He wants to do *(Luke 1:37)*. He placed His Son into Mary's womb by His infinite power.   The holy one to be born was the Son of God. *(Luke 1:34-35)*.

   God intervenes in history now and then, and when He does--and it defies the laws of nature--it's called a miracle. The birth of Jesus was a miracle.

Page 11 and 12 continued:

2. Why are these Triangles and Circles symbols for God?

No one can describe God, but Christians use the **triangle** with three equal sides as one way to understand what we know about God from the Scripture. It represents that God is one Being made up of three distinct Persons who are equal. The Father, Son, and Holy Spirit. We call it the Trinity. That's not a word found in the Bible but it's one way that helps us understand our awesome God. *(Luke 1:35)*

A **circle** is another way to understand what we know about God because it doesn't have a beginning or an end. It represents infinity and eternity. The Father, Son, and Holy Spirit are infinite and eternal. They always have been, and always will be. *(Psalm 90:2)*

Page 13 and 14

1. Why was he named "Jesus"?

The Angel Gabriel told Mary she was to name her son Jesus...that He will be great and will be called the Son of the Most High. *(Luke 1:31-32)* An angel also appeared to Joseph and told him to name the baby Jesus because he will save his people from their sins. *(Matthew 1:21)* Jesus is the Son of God and Savior for all who believe. *(John 3:16)*

2. Wasn't God the creator of the universe?

Genesis 1:1 says that "God created the heavens and the earth." Then, Colossians 1:16 gives the added detail that God created "all things" through Jesus Christ. It's plain, then, from Scripture that it was God's Son, Jesus who created the universe. Remember the Trinity--God the Father, God the Son and God the Holy Spirit.

Page 15 and 16

1. Who is Lucifer?

God created Lucifer to be an angel full of light and beauty and he was known as Star of the Morning, Son of the Dawn. But his heart became proud and corrupt because of his beauty and splendor. He said "I will exalt my throne above the stars of God. I will be like the Most High." So for his proud and corrupt heart, he was kicked out of heaven and thrown to the earth where he is known as the Devil or Satan. *(Ezekiel 28:17, Isaiah 14:12-15)*

The gang of angels who rebelled with him were also kicked out of heaven and are known as demons. They assist him in oppressing and tempting mankind and to separate as many people from God as they can. It's important to remember that the Devil is not equal to the Most High God. The Devil and his demons are only the created beings of the Most High God. He is King over all and has a place of eternal torment prepared for them where they will be thrown at the end of time. *(Revelation 20:10)*

Page 17 and 18

1. Why did the people want to kill Jesus?

Jesus claimed to be, **and is,** the Son of God *(John 8:58)*. His life backed up his claim with miracles like feeding lunch to 5,000 people, healing the sick and even raising someone from the dead. The people were following him and many loved him.   **(Continued on the next page.)**

Page 17 and 18 continued:

But his teaching known as the Beatitudes *(Matthew 5, 6, and 7)* as well as his claim to be the Son of God, angered the religious leaders, because it was so different from their tradition. So they stirred up the people with lies, had Jesus arrested and then sent to the cross and crucified. But this is the very reason he came to earth. He voluntarily died on the cross to be a sacrifice for us, in order to save us from our sins.

Philippians 2:6-8--Christ Jesus, who being in the very nature God, did not consider equality with God something to be grasped, but made himself nothing, taking the very nature of a servant, being made in human likeness, and being found in appearance as a man, he humbled himself and became obedient to death--even death on a cross!

Page 19 and 20

But Hooray! The best part of the story is that 3 days later, Jesus rose from the tomb, triumphant over death just as he told his disciples he would. *(Matthew 17:22-23 and also Mark 9:30-32)*

Mary the mother of Jesus and two other women went to the tomb early in the morning after the Sabbath to anoint Jesus' body. But they found that the tomb was empty (!) and there was an angel sitting nearby who told them "Don't be alarmed." You are looking for Jesus the Nazarene, who was crucified. He is not here. He has risen! *(Mark 16:1-8*

After the resurrection and for about seven weeks, many different people saw him including his mother, the disciples, and a group of over 500 people. *(I Corinthians 15:5-6).*

Then Jesus met with his disciples one last time. When he finished speaking to them he was taken up into heaven where he sat down at the right hand of God. *(Mark 16:19)* His mission was complete.

Page 21 and 22

1. **Who are George Frederic Handel and Johann Sebastian Bach?**
   These are two great composers (who lived over 200 years ago) who wrote incredibly beautiful music that is still loved and sung today.

   George Frederic Handel wrote the **Messiah**, the most frequently performed of all large-scale compositions performed at Christmas and Easter. Scriptures used in the Messiah are from the Old Testament about his birth and the Gospels in the New Testament about his birth, death and resurrection. The ultimate reign of Christ the King is from the Book of Revelation. That is the magnificent and thrilling "Hallelujah Chorus".

   Johann Sebastian Bach has been generally regarded as one of the greatest composers of all time. The anthem he wrote, **"Glory to God in the Highest"** is sometimes abbreviated simply to "Gloria" and we sing it at Christmas. They are the words of the angels when they proclaimed the birth of Jesus to the shepherds.

   Suddenly a great company of the heavenly host appeared with the angel, praising God and saying, "Glory to God in the highest, and on earth peace to men on whom his favor rests." (Luke 2:13-14).

Page 23 and 24

LED light Robes and Wings?

The light shining down on the shepherds from the angels, called the "glory of the Lord" was actually much brighter than our LED lights, probably more like lightening (Luke 24:4). So because this was such an incredible sight, the angel had to say to them, **"Do not be afraid!"**

And there were shepherds living out in the fields nearby, keeping watch over their flocks at night. An angel of the Lord appeared to them and the glory of the Lord shone around them, and they were terrified. But the angel said to them, "Do not be afraid. I bring you good news of great joy that will be for all the people. Today in the city of David a Savior has been born to you; He is Christ the Lord. This will be a sign to you: You will find a baby wrapped in cloths and lying in a manger. Suddenly a great company of the heavenly host appeared with the angel, praising God and saying, "Glory to God in the highest, and on earth peace to men on whom his favor rests." (Luke 2:8-14)

Page 25 and 26

Oh really, Light Robes and Sneakers?

You can read the whole story in the Bible yourself. Luke chapters 1 and 2. *Maybe there are no sneakers.*

Page 27 and 28

How can God's word, the Bible be a treasure chest?

If we spend time reading and thinking about God's word, we find diamonds and rubies of wisdom and truth for our life. God's word becomes more precious than gold (or any of the treasures we love) and sweeter than candy. *(Psalm 19:7-11)*

Page 29 and 30

1. When will Jesus be King of Kings over all the earth?

The answer? At the end of time. Scripture tells us that Jesus, crowned as King of Kings and Lord of Lords, will come out of heaven in the clouds on a white horse at the end of time, to rule and reign over all the earth. *(Revelation 19:11-16)* Because other prophesies in Scripture have all been fulfilled, we can believe this.

2. Who are all those people on horses behind Jesus?

These are the armies of heaven riding on white horses and dressed in white, the faithful followers of Jesus. Some day we'll be on horses that fly? Yes, believers in Jesus will be with him in the clouds of heaven riding on white horses. So exciting!
(Revelation 19:14, Revelation 17:14)

THE STORY: *(Philippians 2:6-11)*
The Cradle--Jesus gave up the glory of heaven to be born as a human.
The Cross--He humbled himself and became obedient unto death, even death on a cross.
The Crown--Therefore God exalted him to the highest place and gave him the name that is above every name, that at the name of Jesus every knee should bow and every tongue confess that Jesus Christ is Lord, to the glory of God the Father.